Clarinet
Sight-reading
from 2018

ABRSM Grades 6-8

Contents

First published in 2017 by ABRSM (Publishing) Ltd, a wholly owned subsidiary of ABRSM
© 2017 by The Associated Board of the Royal Schools of Music
Unauthorized photocopying is illegal

Music origination by Katie Johnston
Cover by Kate Benjamin & Andy Potts
Printed in England by Halstan & Co. Ltd, Amersham, Bucks., on materials from sustainable sources

Grade 6

Sea Swell

1

March Rag

2

Puppets

First Loss

Grade 6

Statement

Animated Waltz

High Fives

A Steady Climb

Grade 6

Time Changes

9

By the River

10

Easy Swing

Five Alive

Grade 6

Up and Away!

13

The Mischievous Gnome

14

Duckling Dance

Andante risoluto

15

mf

f

mp

mf

f

Moving On

Teneramente

16

p

mf

cresc.

f

poco rit.

f

Grade 6

Three-Legged Polka

17 *Andantino*

I've Got a Minor Complaint

18 **Swing**

Jumping Bean

19

Witches' Dance

20

Grade 7

Live Wire

Reflection

Lazy Day

Dance of the Zombies

Grade 7

Ragged Rag

Witches' Waltz

Take Seven

Allegretto comodo

7

mf

p

f

fp *cresc.*

f

Happy Blues

Allegretto ritmico

8

p

mp

f

p

f

p

f

f

mf

ff

Grade 7

Dance of the Ostriches

Go with the Flow

Nocturne

Scherzo in 7

Grade 7

Relaxation

13

Five Go Marching

14

Grade 7

Ghost Dance

15

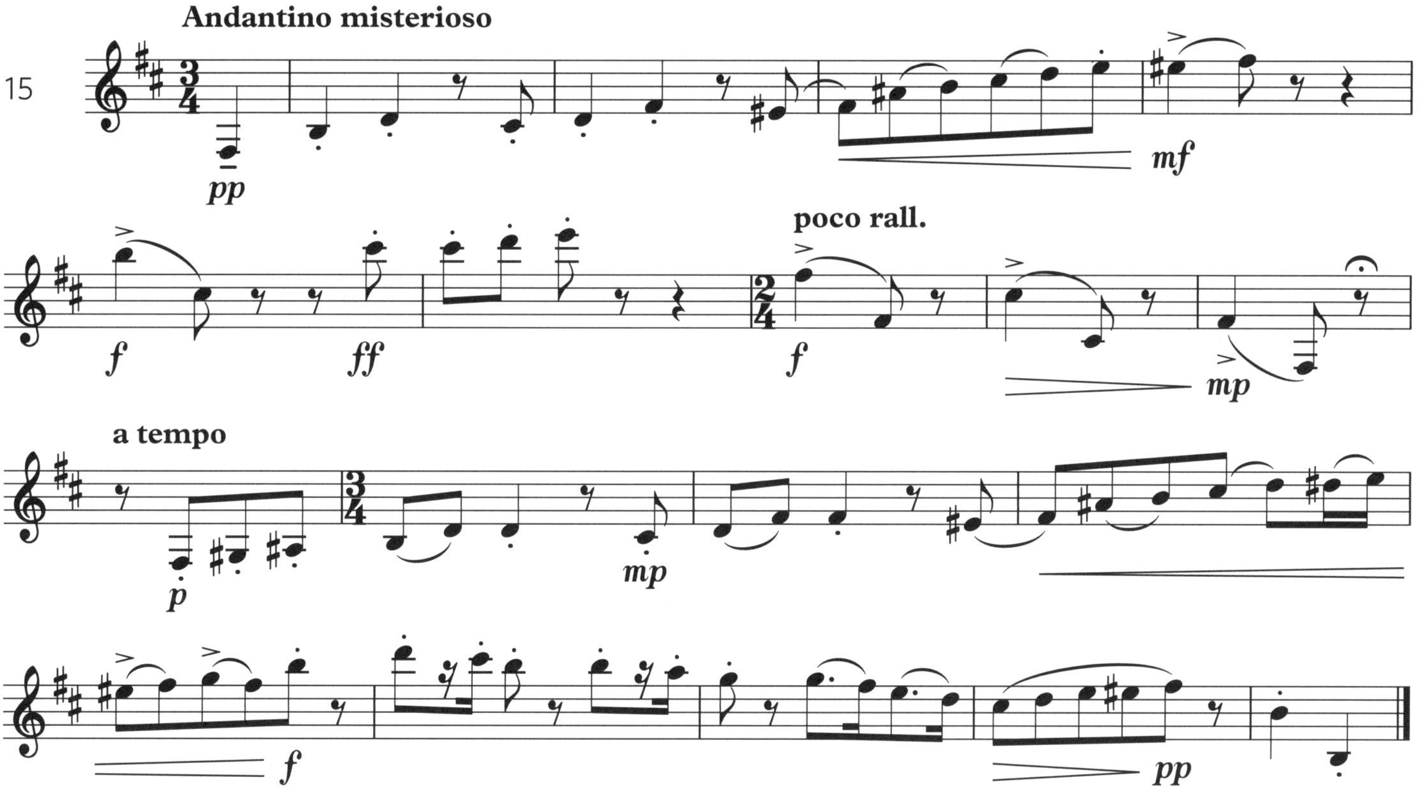

Hornpipe

16

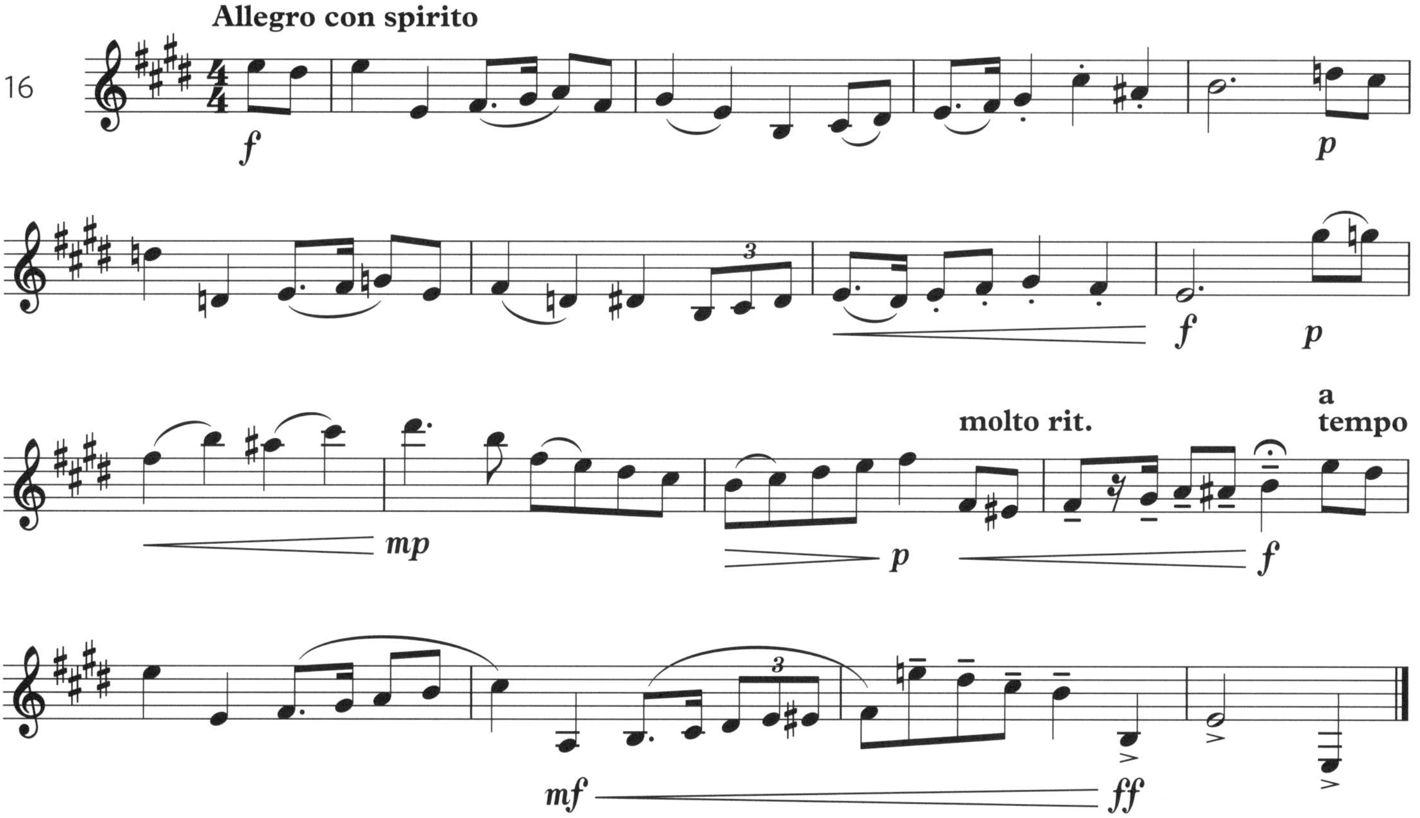

Grade 7

Scamper

Capriccioso

17

Slightly Askew

Vivace

18

Easy Street

19

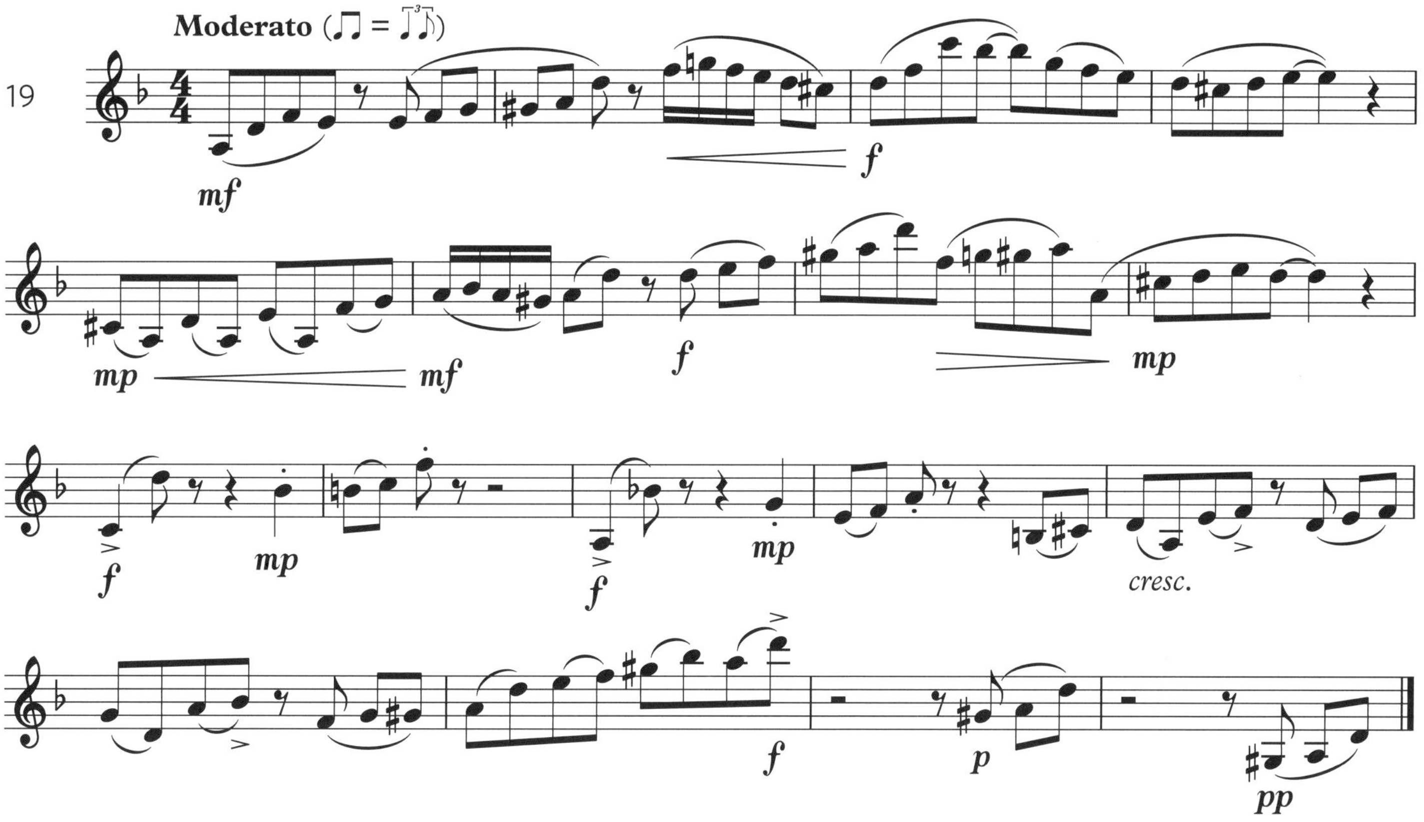

Jolly Jeepers

20

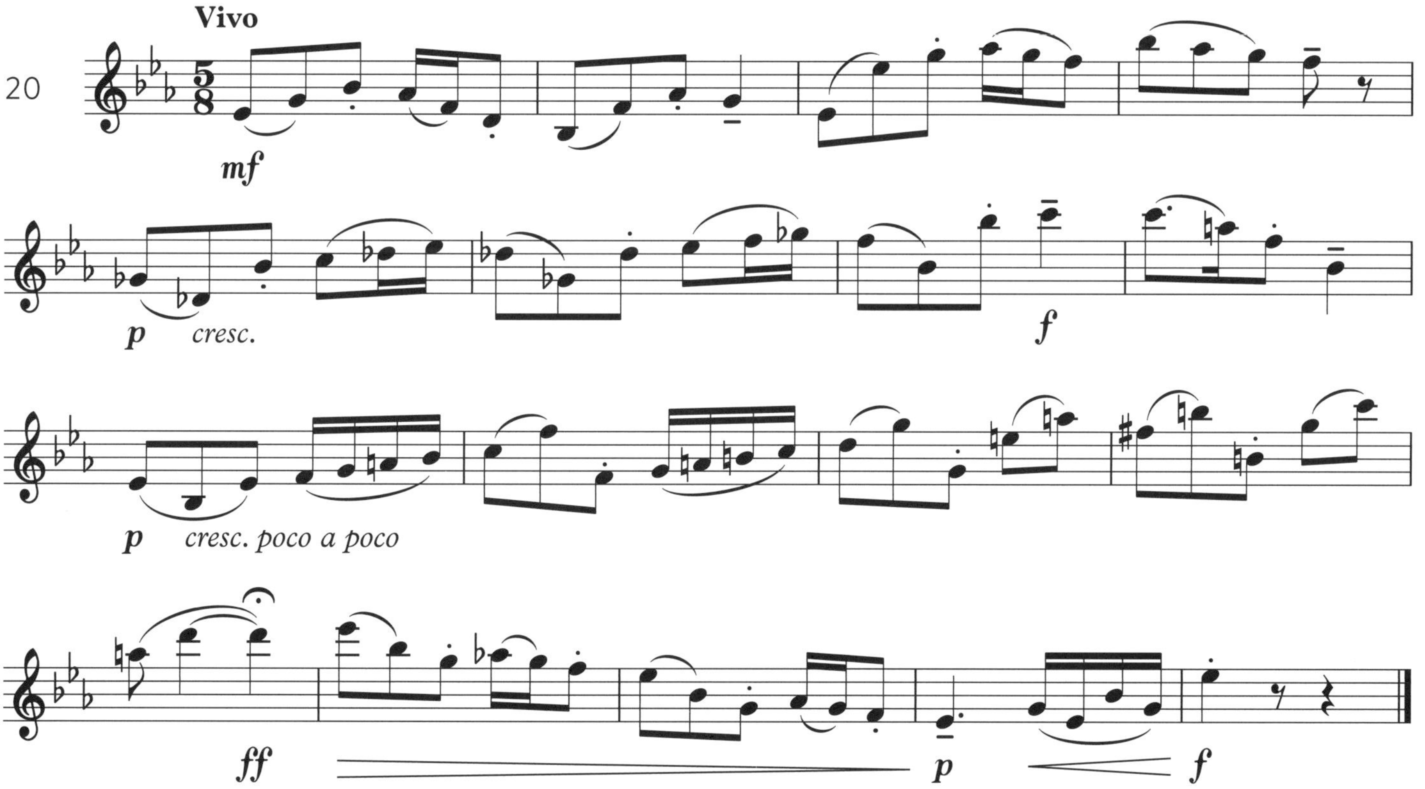

Grade 8

Little Scherzo

Soft-Shoe Shuffle

Helter-skelter

Sail Away

Grade 8

Wayward Waltz

Fairground

Grade 8

Memories of Long Ago

7

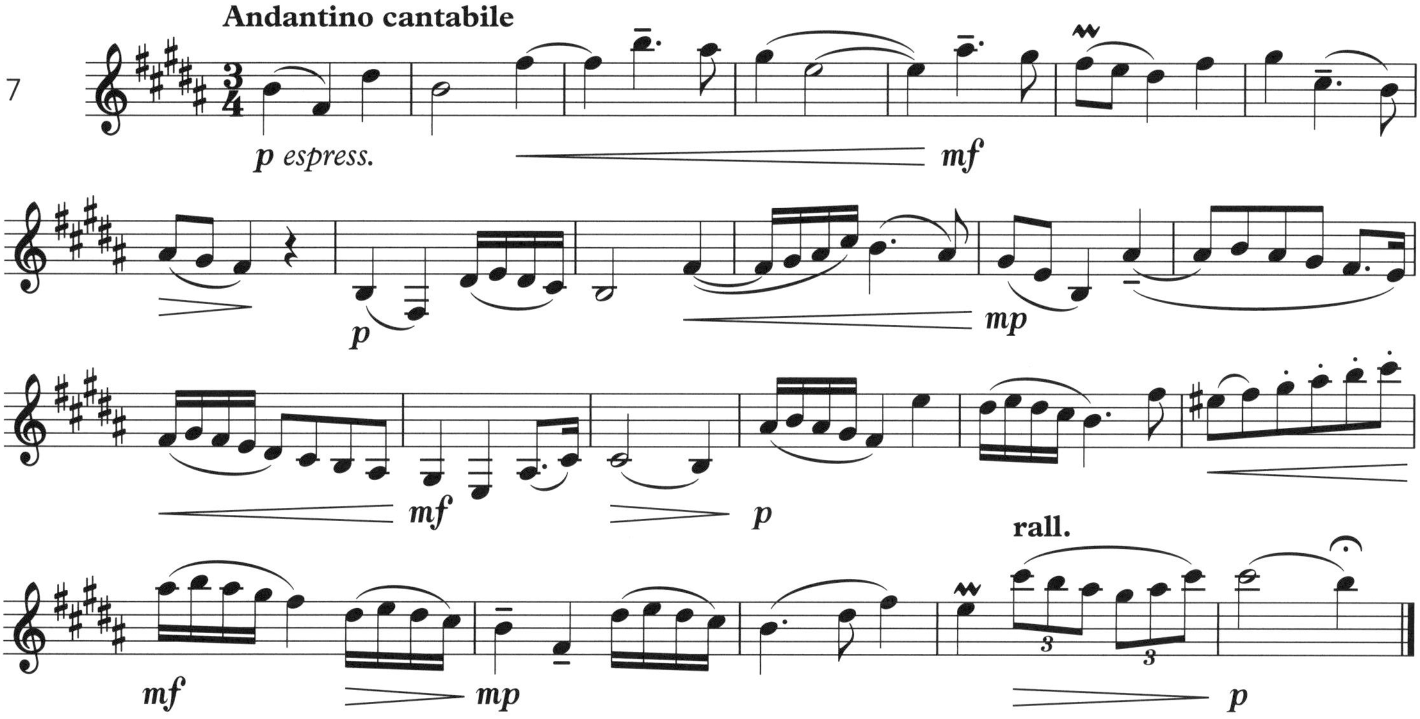

Sicilienne

8

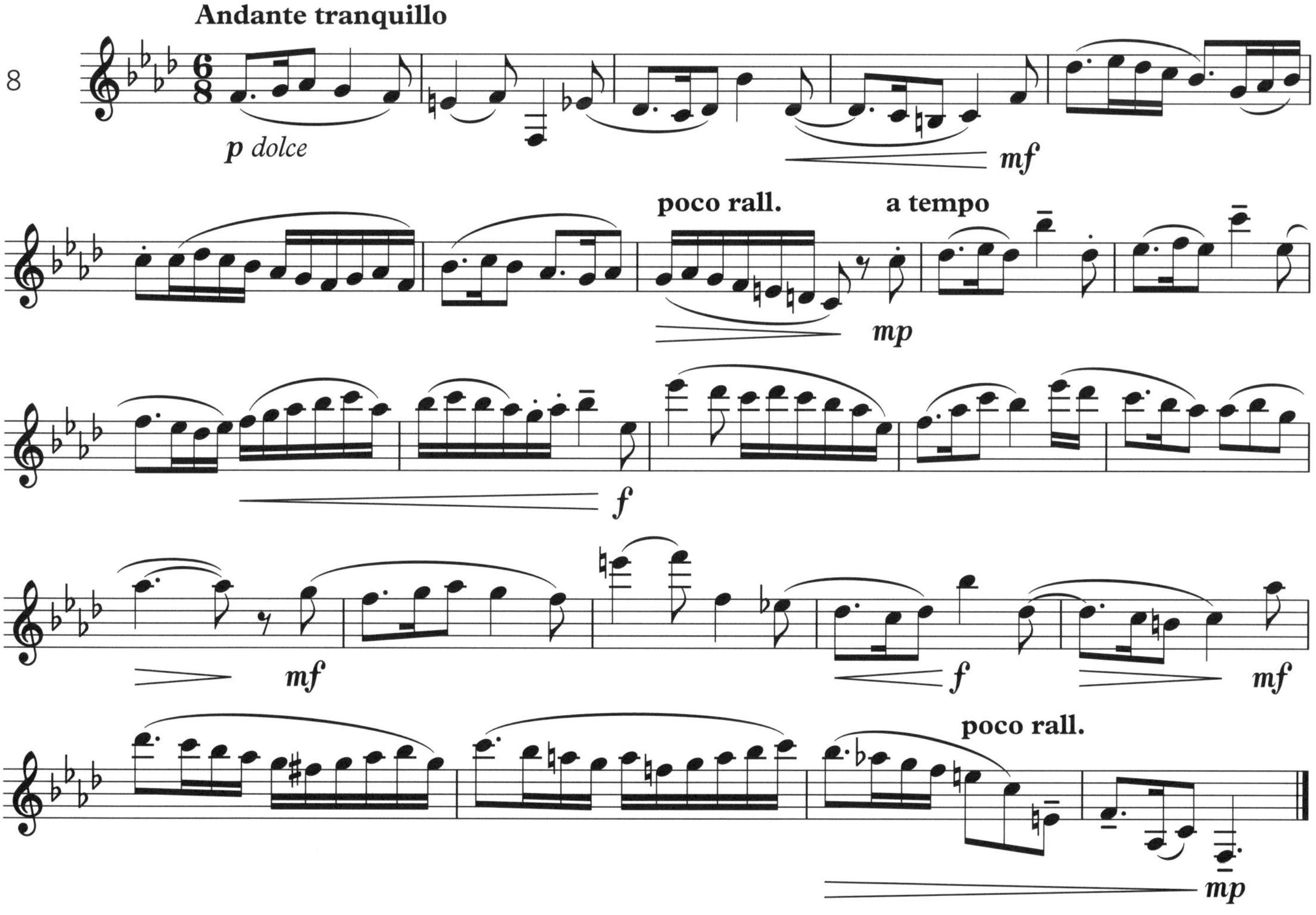

Grade 8

Ragtime Romp

Allegretto ritmico

9

Blue Funk

Con anima

10

Grade 8

Hippos on Parade

11

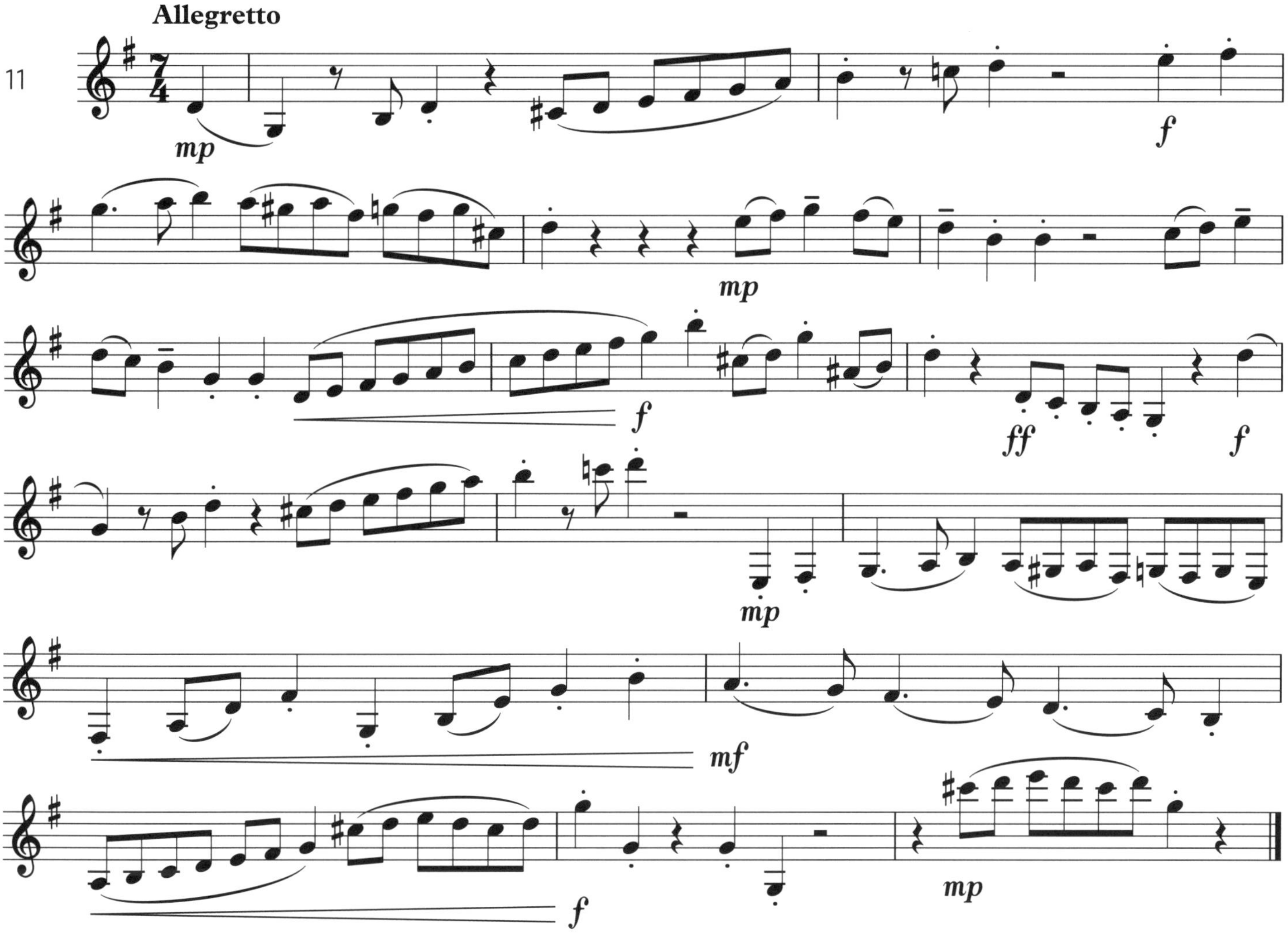

Highland Stroll

12

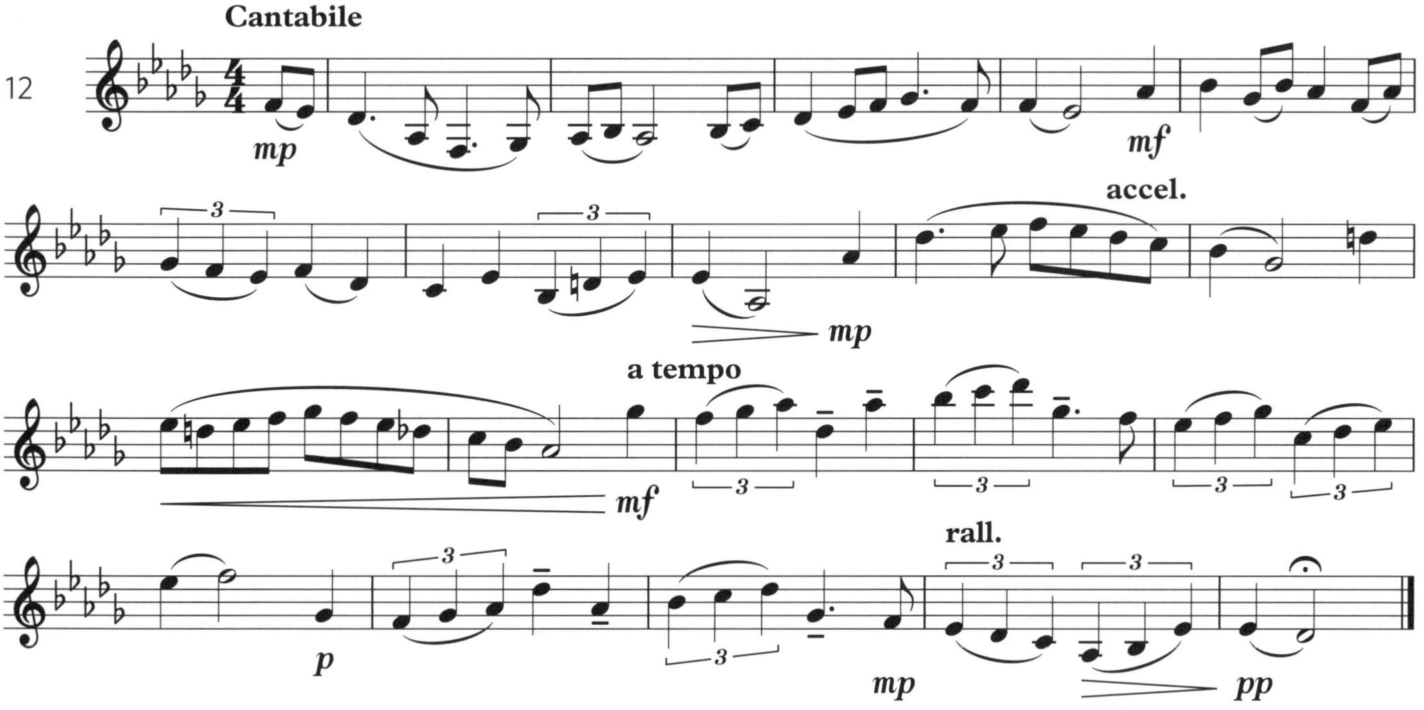

Grade 8

Rock Face

Molto ritmico

13

My Homeland

Larghetto amabile

14

The Missing Link

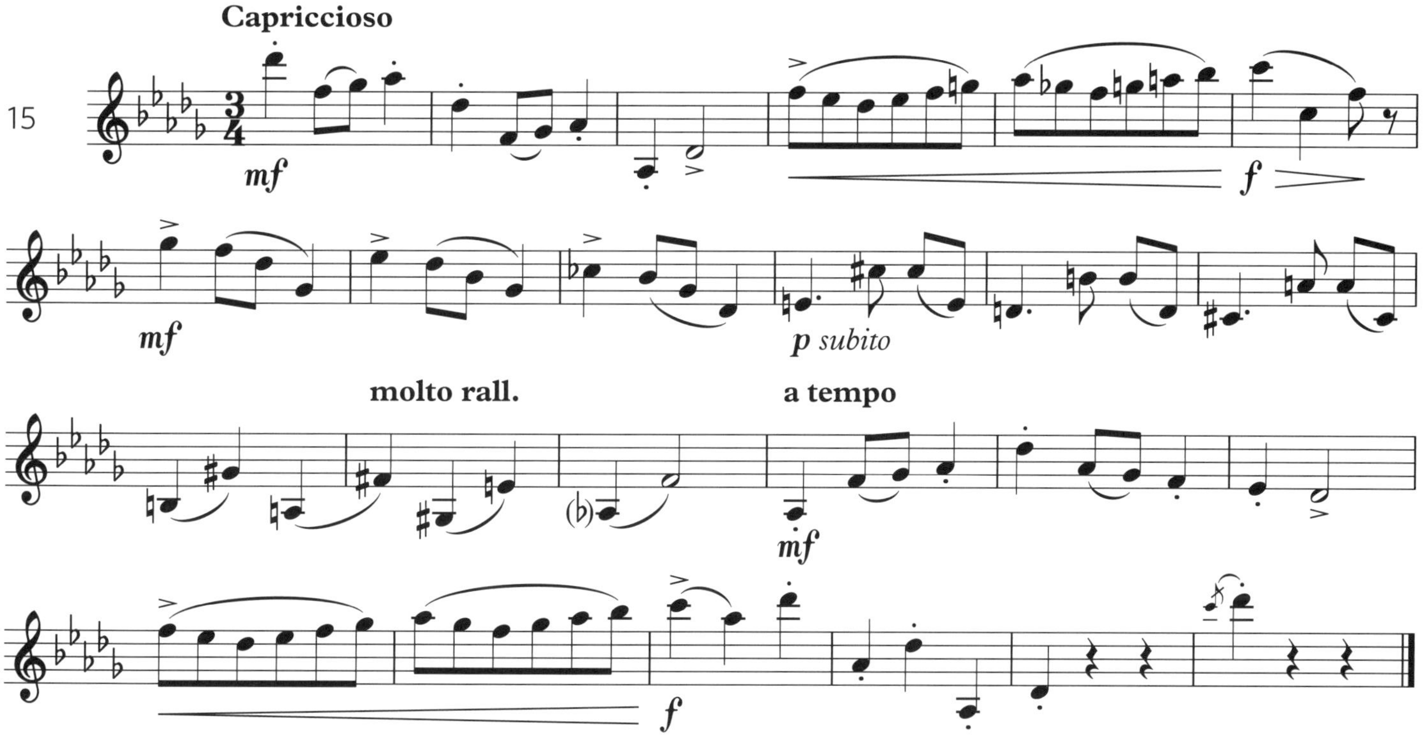

Seventh Heaven

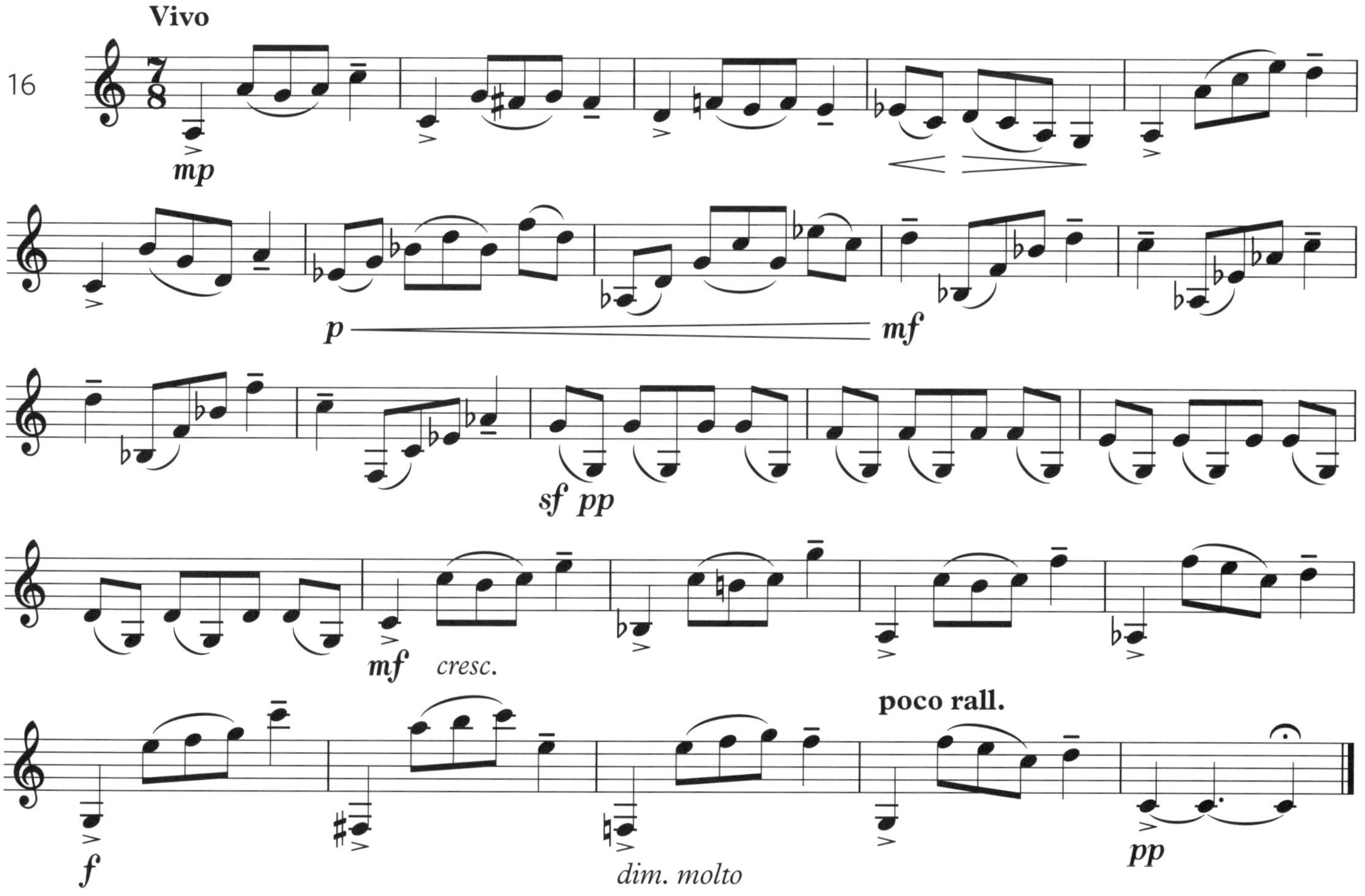

Grade 8

Serenade

Oriental Dance

Swing It!

Energico (♩♩ = ♩³♪)

19

Chromatic Caprice

Andante con moto

20